New Careers for the
21st Century:
Finding Your Role in
the Global Renewal

PHYSICIANS'
ASSISTANTS & NURSES:

NEW OPPORTUNITIES IN THE
21ST-CENTURY HEALTH SYSTEM

WEST BEND LIBRARY

New Careers for the 21st Century: Finding Your Role in the Global Renewal

New Careers for the
21st Century:
Finding Your Role in
the Global Renewal

PHYSICIANS'
ASSISTANTS & NURSES:

NEW OPPORTUNITIES IN THE
21ST-CENTURY HEALTH SYSTEM

by Cordelia Strange

Mason Crest Publishers

PHYSICIANS' ASSISTANTS & NURSES:
NEW OPPORTUNITIES IN THE 21ST-CENTURY HEALTH SYSTEM

Copyright © 2011 by Mason Crest Publishers. All rights reserved. No part of this publication may be reproduced or transmitted in any form or by any means, electronic or mechanical, including photocopying, recording, taping, or any information storage and retrieval system, without permission from the publisher.

MASON CREST PUBLISHERS INC.
370 Reed Road
Broomall, Pennsylvania 19008
(866)MCP-BOOK (toll free)
www.masoncrest.com

First Printing
9 8 7 6 5 4 3 2 1

Library of Congress Cataloging-in-Publication Data

Strange, Cordelia.
  Physicians' assistants & nurses : new opportunities in the 21st-century health system / by Cordelia Strange.
      p. cm.
  Includes bibliographical references and index.
  ISBN 978-1-4222-1820-4   ISBN 978-1-4222-1811-2 (series)
  ISBN 978-1-4222-2041-2 (ppb)   ISBN 978-1-4222-2032-0 (series pbb)
  1. Physicians' assistants—Juvenile literature. 2. Nurses—Juvenile literature. I. Title. II. Title: Physicians assistants and nurses.
  R697.P45S77 2011
  610.73'72069—dc22
                                                2010017919

Produced by Harding House Publishing Service, Inc.
www.hardinghousepages.com
Interior Design by MK Bassett-Harvey.
Cover design by Torque Advertising + Design.
Printed in USA by Bang Printing.

CONTENTS

YA
331.702
P5680

INTRODUCTION

Be careful as you begin to plan your career.

To get yourself in the best position to begin the career of your dreams, you need to know what the "green world" will look like and what jobs will be created and what jobs will become obsolete. Just think, according to the Bureau of Labor Statistics, the following jobs are expected to severely decline by 2012:

- word processors and data-entry keyers

- stock clerks and order fillers

- secretaries

- electrical and electronic equipment assemblers

- computer operators

- telephone operators

- postal service mail sorters and processing-machine operators

- travel agents

These are just a few of the positions that will decrease or become obsolete as we move forward into the century.

You need to know what the future jobs will be. How do you find them? One way is to look where money is being invested. Many firms and corporations are now making investments in startup and research enterprises. These companies may become the "Microsoft" and "Apple" of the twenty-first century. Look at what is being researched and what technology is needed to obtain the results.

Green world, green economy, green technology—they all say the same things: the way we do business today is changing. Every industry will be shaped by the world's new focus on creating a sustainable lifestyle, one that won't deplete our natural and economic resources.

The possibilities are unlimited. Almost any area that will conserve energy and reduce the dependency on fossil fuels is open to new and exciting career paths. Many of these positions have not even been identified yet and will only come to light as the technology progresses and new discoveries are made in the way we use that technology. And the best part about this is that our government is behind us. The U.S. government wants to help you get the education and training you'll need to succeed and grow in this new and changing economy. The U.S. Department of Labor has launched a series of initiatives to support and promote green job creation. To view the report, visit: www.dol.gov/dol/green/earthday_reportA.pdf.

The time to decide on your future is now. This series, New Careers for the 21st Century: Finding Your Role in the Global Renewal, can act as the first step toward your continued education, training, and career path decisions. Take the first steps that will lead you—and the planet—to a productive and sustainable future.

Mike Puglisi
Department of Labor, District I Director (New York/New Jersey)
IAWP (International Association of Workforce Professionals)

*One learns
through the
heart, not the
eyes or the
intellect.*

—Mark Twain

ABOUT THE QUOTE

As you think about what you want to do in life, your grades and aptitudes may help shape your career goals. But also pay attention to your emotions. What moves you? What excites you? What are the things you care about most? Those are the things that will likely keep you committed to whatever career you choose, more than prestige or salary.

CHAPTER 1
WHAT DO PHYSICIAN ASSISTANTS AND NURSES DO?

WORDS TO KNOW

epidemiologist: A scientist who studies the sources, appearance of, and amount of disease in large populations.

diagnostic: Having to do with the diagnosis of illness or problems—in other words, figuring out what's wrong.

therapeutic: Related to the healing of disease.

pediatrics: The branch of medicine dealing with children and adolescents.

orthopedics: The branch of medicine dealing with injuries or problems with the skeleton, muscles, and ligaments.

geriatrics: The branch of medicine dealing with elderly patients.

perioperative: Having to do with the period around the time of a surgery.

obstetrical: Having to do with childbirth.

neonatal: Having to do with babies during the first month after their birth.

What comes to mind when you think of medicine? Do you picture a surgeon poised over a table in an operating room, or a family doctor caring for patients in an office? While doctors dominate many popular images of the medical industry, they are not the only option for a student interested in a health care career. Dentist, pharmacist, medical technician, veterinarian, and *epidemiologist* are just some of the many other career options available in the health-care industry. There are also many healthcare workers who assist and support doctors and surgeons. These people are vital to the healthcare industry, even if they do not always get the glory of a doctor. Physician assistant and nurse are two of these careers. Both offer assistance and support to doctors, and perform many tests and tasks you might normally associate with your doctor.

> **Did You Know?**
> Registered nurses (RNs) are the largest healthcare occupation, with 2.6 million jobs.

CHOOSING THE RIGHT CAREER

The young adults of today will be the job force of tomorrow, so choosing a career that will best fit with the needs of the changing world will be important to job satisfaction and a successful life. With the vast array of career and job options, it is important for young adults to understand which work will be the best match for their interests, talents, goals, and personality types. If you enjoy working with people and are interested in a career in medicine

but do not want to be a doctor, then a career as a physician's assistant or nurse might be a good choice.

Certain job industries are expected to gain importance within the early decades of the twenty-first century. The opportunities for medical careers in general are expected to increase at a faster than average rate. According to the United States Bureau of Labor Statistics, the number of jobs across all industries is expected to increase by 11 percent through the year 2018. The number of jobs is expected to increase by 39 percent for physician assistants and 22 percent for nurses.

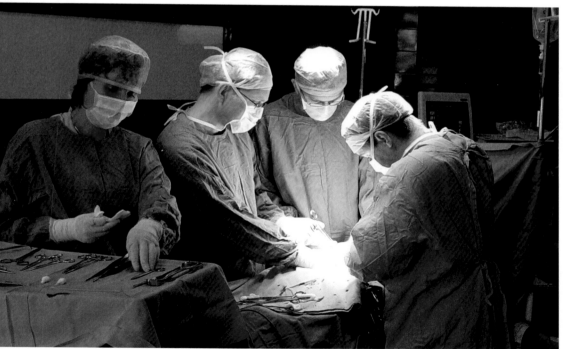

An operation usually involves a lot of people, doing many different tasks. Only a couple of these people are doctors—the rest might be medical technicians, nurses, or physician assistants.

PHYSICIAN ASSISTANTS

Physician assistants (PAs) practice medicine under the supervision of physicians and surgeons. PAs are trained to provide *diagnostic*, *therapeutic*, and preventive care, as directed by a physician. Physician assistants basically do all the same tasks as doctors. They take medical histories, examine and treat patients, order and read laboratory tests and X-rays, and make diagnoses. They also treat minor injuries. PAs create case reports, instruct and counsel patients, and order or carry out therapy. Physician assistants can also prescribe some medications. Sometimes, a PA is responsible for ordering medical supplies or equipment and supervising medical technicians and assistants.

Usually, physician assistants work under a physician, but in some rural or inner-city areas, they may be responsible for more of patients' care. In these locations, doctors are only present one or two days a week, so the PAs care for patients and consult with the doctor as needed or required by law. These physician assistants may also make house calls, check on patients in hospitals or nursing homes, and report back to the doctor about these patients.

Many physician assistants work in specialty areas such as internal medicine, *pediatrics*, family medicine, surgery, emergency medicine, *orthopedics*, and *geriatrics*.
PAs specializing in surgery provide patient care before and after surgery, or they may work as assistants during surgery.

The supervising physician decides on the duties of a physician assistant, but there are also guidelines and restrictions based on state law. Each state has different laws, so if you are interested in a career as a PA, check the specific laws and regulations of the state in which you hope to practice.

WORK ENVIRONMENT

Although physician assistants usually work in a comfortable, well-lighted environment, those in surgery often stand for long periods of time. Also, at times, the job may require a lot of walking. Work schedules will vary by work setting, and often depend on the hours worked by the supervising physician.

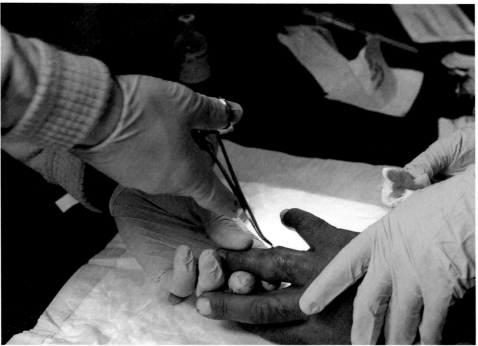

Physician assistants assist doctors during surgery, and sometimes perform minor tasks, like stitches on their own.

NURSES

Nurses, also known as registered nurses (RNs), treat patients, educate patients and the public, and provide advice and support to patients and families. RNs take medical histories, record patient symptoms, perform tests and analyze results, operate medical equipment, administer treatment, give medications, and help with patient follow-up and rehabilitation.

Education is an important part of a nurse's job. RNs teach patients and their families how to manage illness or injury. They explain home-care needs, diet and exercise programs, and proper administration of medication. Some nurses are active in public health-care education, teaching the general public the warning signs and symptoms of disease. RNs also run general health screening or immunization clinics, blood drives, and public classes.

When caring for patients, RNs establish or contribute to a routine or plan. Plans include numerous activities, such as giving medication; starting, maintaining, and removing intravenous (IV) lines; administering therapies and treatments; observing the patient and recording those observations; and consulting with physicians and other health-care clinicians. Some RNs supervise licensed practical nurses and nursing aides. RNs with advanced education and training may perform diagnostic and therapeutic procedures and may be allowed to write prescriptions.

A nurse's specific duties vary depending on work setting, patient population, or specialization. RNs can specialize in four ways: by type of treatment, by health condition, by body system/organ, or by population. Many RNs combine multiple specialties; for example, pediatric oncology nurses deal with children and adolescents who have cancer. The opportunities for specialization in registered nursing are widely varied and are often determined on the job.

NURSE SPECIALIZATIONS

TYPE OF TREATMENT SPECIALIZATIONS

There are many treatment specializations, including the following:

- Critical-care nurses provide care to patients with serious, complex, and acute illnesses or injuries.

- Emergency nurses, also known as trauma nurses, work in hospital or stand-alone emergency departments.

- Holistic nurses provide care such as acupuncture, massage and aromatherapy, and biofeedback, which are meant to treat patients' mental and spiritual health in addition to their physical health.

- *Perioperative* nurses assist surgeons by selecting and handling instruments, controlling bleeding, and suturing incisions.

- Radiology nurses provide care to patients undergoing diagnostic radiation procedures such as ultrasounds, magnetic resonance imaging, and radiation therapy for oncology diagnoses.

HEALTH CONDITION SPECIALIZATION

RNs specializing in a particular disease, ailment, or healthcare condition are employed in virtually all work settings, including physicians' offices, outpatient treatment facilities, home health-care agencies, and hospitals. Among others, these nurses include:

- Addictions nurses care for patients seeking help with alcohol, drug, tobacco, and other addictions.

- Intellectual and developmental disabilities nurses provide care for patients with physical, mental, or behavioral disabilities.

- Genetics nurses provide early detection screenings, counseling, and treatment of patients with genetic disorders, including cystic fibrosis and Huntington's disease.

- Oncology nurses care for patients with various types of cancer and may assist in the administration of radiation and chemotherapies and follow-up monitoring.

BODY SYSTEM OR ORGAN SPECIALIZATION

RNs specializing in treatment of a particular organ or body system usually are employed in hospital specialty or critical-care units, specialty clinics, and outpatient care facilities. Organ or body system specializations include:

- Cardiovascular nurses treat patients with coronary heart disease and those who have had heart surgery, providing services such as postoperative rehabilitation.

- Gynecology nurses provide care to women with disorders of the reproductive system, including endometriosis, cancer, and sexually transmitted diseases.

- Neuroscience nurses care for patients with dysfunctions of the nervous system, including brain and spinal cord injuries, and seizures.

- Orthopedic nurses care for patients with muscular and skeletal problems, including arthritis, bone fractures, and muscular dystrophy.

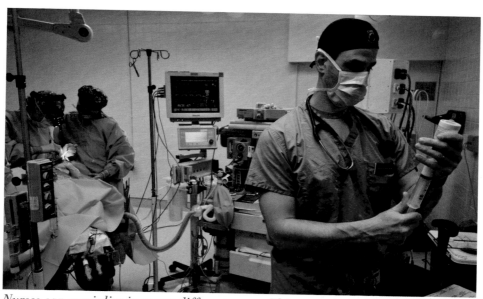

Nurses can specialize in many different areas. This nurse is an anesthesiologist—he makes sure the patient receives the right dose of anesthesia and then monitors the patient's vital signs during surgery.

POPULATION SPECIALIZATION

RNs who specialize by population provide preventive and acute care in all health-care settings to the segment of the population in which they specialize, including:

- newborns (neonatology)

- children and adolescents (pediatrics)

- adults

- the elderly (gerontology or geriatrics)

These nurses may also provide basic healthcare to patients outside healthcare settings, including correctional facilities, schools, summer camps, and the military. Some nurses travel throughout the world providing care to patients in areas with shortages of health-care workers.

ADVANCED PRACTICE NURSES

Some nurses become advanced practice nurses, who work independently or in collaboration with physicians, and may focus on the provision of primary care services. There are four types of advanced practice nurses:

- Clinical nurse specialists provide direct patient care and expert consultations in one of many nursing specialties, such as psychiatric-mental health.

- Nurse anesthetists provide anesthesia and related care before and after surgical, therapeutic, diagnostic, and *obstetrical* procedures.

- Nurse-midwives provide primary care to women, including gynecological exams, family planning advice, prenatal care, assistance in labor and delivery, and *neonatal* care.

- Nurse practitioners serve as primary and specialty care providers, providing a blend of nursing and healthcare services to patients and families in areas like family practice, adult practice, women's health, pediatrics, acute care, and geriatrics.

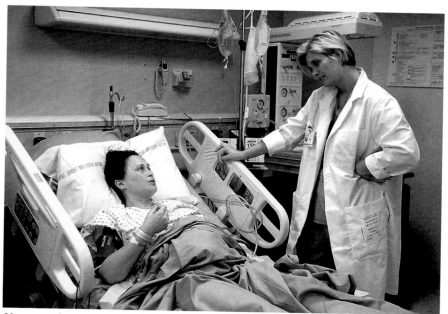

Nurse midwives work in the field of female health, including gynecology and obstetrics. This nurse midwife is checking on a pregnant patient before her scheduled cesarean-section.

Advanced practice nurses can prescribe medications in all states and in the District of Columbia.

LIMITED PATIENT CARE

Some nurses have jobs that require little or no direct patient care, but still require an active RN license. For example:

- Forensics nurses participate in the scientific investigation and treatment of abuse victims, violence, criminal activity, and traumatic accidents.

- Infection control nurses identify, track, and control infectious outbreaks in healthcare facilities and develop programs for outbreak prevention and response to biological terrorism.

- Nurse educators plan, develop, implement, and evaluate educational programs and curricula for the professional development of student nurses and RNs.

   RNs also may work as healthcare consultants, public policy advisors, pharmaceutical and medical supply researchers and salespersons, and medical writers and editors.

WORK ENVIRONMENT

Nurses often work in close contact with patients who have infectious diseases and with potentially hazardous compounds, solutions, and medications. As a result, nurses must follow rigid, standardized guidelines to guard against disease and other dangers. In addition, many nurses spend a lot of time on their feet and are prone to back injury when moving patients.

What Kind of Person Are You?

Career-counseling experts know that certain kinds of people do best in certain kinds of jobs. John L. Holland developed the following list of personality types and the kinds of jobs that are the best match for each type. See which one (or two) are most like you. The more you understand yourself, the better you'll be able to make a good career plan for yourself.

- **Realistic personality**: This kind of person likes to do practical, hands-on work. He or she will most enjoy working with materials that can be touched and manipulated, such as wood, steel, tools, and machinery. This personality type enjoys jobs that require working outdoors, but he or she does NOT enjoy jobs that require a lot of paperwork or close teamwork with others.

- **Investigative personality**: This personality type likes to work with ideas. He or she will enjoy jobs that require lots of thinking and researching. Jobs that require mental problem solving will be a good fit for this personality.

- **Artistic personality**: This type of person enjoys working with forms, designs, and patterns. She or he likes jobs that require self-expression—and that don't require following a definite set of rules.

- **Social personality**: Jobs that require lots of teamwork with others, as well as teaching others, are a good match for this personality type. These jobs often involve helping others in some way.

- **Enterprising personality**: This person will enjoy planning and starting new projects, even if that involves a degree of risk-taking. He or she is good at making decisions and leading others.

- **Conventional personality**: An individual with this type of personality likes to follow a clear set of procedures or routines. He or she doesn't want to be the boss but prefers to work under someone else's leadership. Jobs that require working with details and facts (more than ideas) are a good fit for this personality.

Make your work to be in keeping with your purpose.

—Leonardo da Vinci

ABOUT THE QUOTE

Do you ever think about why you exist? Do you believe you were created to excel at whatever you do? Or do you find your reason for existence in your ability to help others? Or both? If you had your choice, which would you choose to do: make a million dollars—or discover a way to diminish human suffering? Finding honest answers to these questions are important steppingstones toward discovering the right career for you. You will probably never be rich from the salary you earn as either a nurse or a PA—so if your purpose in life is to make money, this is not the right career for you! But if you want to make a difference in the health and well-being of individuals, these careers are options you might want to consider.

CHAPTER 2
THE IMPORTANCE OF PAs AND NURSES

WORDS TO KNOW

demographics: Statistical data about a population and the types of groups within the population.

life expectancy: The number of years an individual is likely to live.

fertility rates: The average number of births per woman in a population.

baby boomers: The generation of people born in the years following World War II, when there was an increase in birthrate.

longevity: Length of life.

policy: A course of action followed by a government.

We live in a constantly changing world. Climate change is threatening our environment and health, new advances in technology make cars more environmentally friendly, computers and cell phones keep friends and family close through virtual connections, and science is always discovering new ways to battle

illness or extend life. With this constant flux, are there any pre-
dictions we can make about what the future will be like?

We may not be able to paint an exact picture of what the future
will bring, but there are some things we can predict. One thing

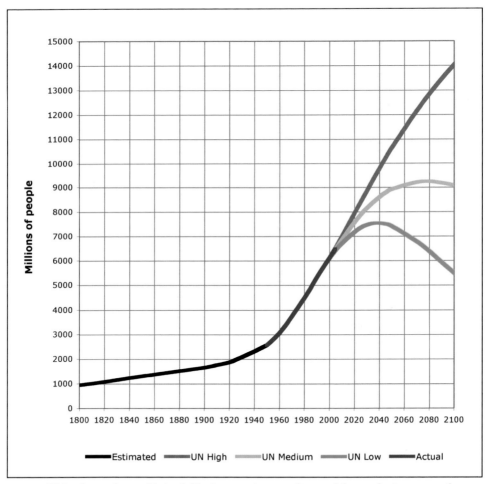

*This chart shows United Nations estimates for world population growth
through 2100.*

that most experts consider a fact is that more people will be living on the planet in the future. The world population is currently at almost 7 million, and it is expected to grow to almost 10 billion by 2050. This growing population, combined with changing *demographics*, will lead to a greater need for health-care workers like physician assistants and nurses.

WHY IS THE POPULATION AGING?

According to the World Health Organization, the fastest growing segment in almost all countries is the over-sixty age group. This is due to a combination of increased *life expectancy* and lower *fertility rates*. According to the United States Census Bureau, the world's sixty-five and older population is projected to triple by midcentury, from 516 million in 2009 to 1.53 billion in 2050. In contrast, the population under fifteen is expected to increase by only 6 percent during the same period, from 1.83 billion to 1.93 billion.

Did You Know?
The total population of the United States is currently about 308,000,000.

The entire world is seeing an increase in this discrepancy between the older and younger generations. For example, in the United States, the population sixty-five and older is expected to more than double by 2050, rising from 39 million today to 89 million, but the under-fifteen population in the United States is expected to fall below the older population by that date, only increasing from 62 million today to 85 million.

Since 1998, the number of older Americans has increased by 13 percent, which is only slightly faster than the 12.4 percent increase for the under-sixty-five population.

The concern for the future is that the *baby boomers* in the forty-five- to sixty-four-year-old age group (who will reach sixty-five over the next two decades) increased by 31 percent since 1998. Also, the "oldest old," the age group of eighty and

Did You Know?
Since 1900, the percentage of Americans over 65 years old has tripled, from 4.1% in 1900 to 12.8% in 2008.

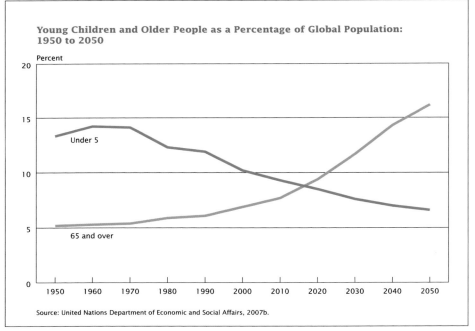

Young Children and Older People as a Percentage of Global Population: 1950 to 2050

Source: United Nations Department of Economic and Social Affairs, 2007b.

While the number of people 65 and older is projected to increase in the coming decades, the number of children under five is expected to decrease. Overall, this will contribute to an increase in the average age of the world's population.

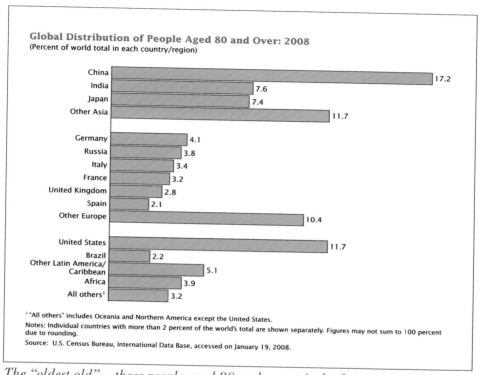

Global Distribution of People Aged 80 and Over: 2008
(Percent of world total in each country/region)

Country/Region	Percent
China	17.2
India	7.6
Japan	7.4
Other Asia	11.7
Germany	4.1
Russia	3.8
Italy	3.4
France	3.2
United Kingdom	2.8
Spain	2.1
Other Europe	10.4
United States	11.7
Brazil	2.2
Other Latin America/Caribbean	5.1
Africa	3.9
All others[1]	3.2

[1] "All others" includes Oceania and Northern America except the United States.
Notes: Individual countries with more than 2 percent of the world's total are shown separately. Figures may not sum to 100 percent due to rounding.
Source: U.S. Census Bureau, International Data Base, accessed on January 19, 2008.

The "oldest old"—those people aged 80 and over—is the fastest growing segment of the population around the world.

over, is increasing more rapidly than the older population as a whole. In other words, the population of the United States—and the entire world—is aging.

WHY IS AN AGING POPULATION A PUBLIC HEALTH CONCERN?

So why is an aging population considered a public health problem? You might think instead that it's a public health success (since people are staying alive longer than ever before). In some ways, this increased *longevity* does represent human triumphs over disease and disaster. However, the shift in population age from a young population to an older one has many implications for public health care and *policy*.

Did You Know?
There were 92,127 persons who were 100 or more in the United States alone in 2008!

Part of the public health concern has to do with the fact that an aging population will experience different types of illnesses. Older people are more likely to be troubled by chronic diseases, such as heart disease, cancer, and diabetes. Therefore an increase in the older population will equal an increase in chronic disease. In fact, according to the National Institute on Aging, in the next ten to fifteen years, the loss of health and life around the world will be greater from chronic diseases than from infectious or parasitic diseases.

The family structure and economic status of the aging generation also pose a public health concern. Lower fertility rates combined with the increase in an older population and the simultaneous reduction in the younger population will leave an increased number of older people alone in their final years. Traditionally, children or grandchildren cared for older people in their declining years. However, in the future, many of the older generation will not have children or grandchildren to provide this care. In addition, increased rates of divorce and separation will leave many older men and women without a system of monetary or social support. Non-married older women are less likely to have accumulated wealth for use in old age, while non-married older men are less likely to have formed a strong social support system.

All these issues will lead to a need for increased public support for the older generation. An increased number of health service centers will be needed to provide care to the older population.

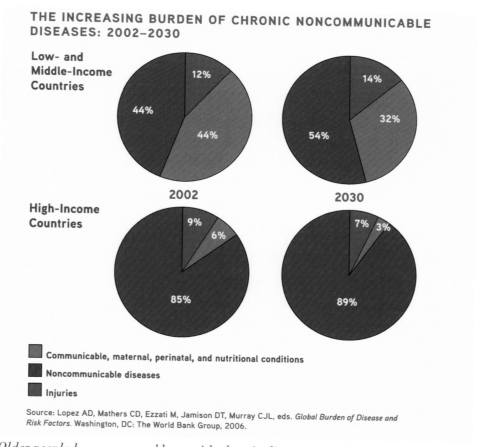

THE INCREASING BURDEN OF CHRONIC NONCOMMUNICABLE DISEASES: 2002–2030

Low- and Middle-Income Countries

2002: 12%, 44%, 44%
2030: 14%, 32%, 54%

High-Income Countries

2002: 9%, 6%, 85%
2030: 7%, 3%, 89%

Communicable, maternal, perinatal, and nutritional conditions
Noncommunicable diseases
Injuries

Source: Lopez AD, Mathers CD, Ezzati M, Jamison DT, Murray CJL, eds. *Global Burden of Disease and Risk Factors*. Washington, DC: The World Bank Group, 2006.

Older people have more problems with chronic diseases, which require constant monitoring and more long-term care than infectious diseases. As the disease burden of the world shifts toward chronic diseases, more health-care workers will be needed to provide the necessary services.

Chronic diseases require regular monitoring to prevent negative effects on the overall quality of life. Also, the increase in older people who are without family support may require an increase in the number of long-term nursing care facilities.

Needed: More Health-Care Workers

The increase in an older population will result in an overall increase in the demand for health-care workers. For example, according to the United States Department of Health and Human Services, if health-care consumption patterns and physician productivity remain constant over time, the aging population would increase the need for physicians per thousand people from 2.8 in 2000 to 3.1 in 2020; demand for RNs per thousand people would increase from 7 to 7.5 during this same period. It is not only doctors and nurses who will be needed; projected employment growth is expected to

Did You Know?
China has the largest older population—106 million in 2008. Japan is the "oldest" country, with 22% of its population 65 or older.

be excellent for all divisions in the health-care industry. In fact, this increase in the need for health care is expected to create a demand for more cost-effective health-care workers, such as physician assistants. As a result of the projected growth in both these fields, a young student considering a career as a nurse or physician assistant can look forward to excellent job opportunities in the future.

If You Have a Social Personality . . .

Health care is an ideal field for you to pursue. PA and nursing positions will give you many opportunities to help people who need you. Since you're genuinely and warmly interested in people and their problems, these careers will keep you constantly interested in your work life—and that's a good thing!

If You Have a Conventional Personality . . .

You might like working in a nursing or PA position where you are directly supervised by a doctor or other superior. Your ability to follow directions in an orderly way will be an asset to you in a position like this—but you might feel overwhelmed in a nursing or PA position where you would have more decision-making responsibilities.

Learning can be defined as the process of remembering what you are interested in.

—Richard Saul Wurman

ABOUT THE QUOTE

At this point in your life, you may feel tired of going to school. But you will soon be at the point in your life where you will get to choose the things you study. Take time to discover what really interests you, and the process of preparing for your career will be both exciting and fulfilling.

CHAPTER 3
EDUCATION AND TRAINING

WORDS TO KNOW

accredited: Officially authorized after certain standards are met.

clinical: Related to the instruction that includes the observation and/or treatment of actual patients, as opposed to classroom, laboratory, or theoretical studies.

master's degree: The degree awarded to a student who has completed at least one year of graduate study.

bachelor's degree: The degree given to a student who completes four years of undergraduate studies.

associate's degree: The degree given to a student who completes two years of study; usually given by community colleges.

liberal arts: The subjects included in a general education: literature, philosophy, mathematics, and social and physical sciences.

ambulatory: Capable of walking; ambulatory health-care centers care for patients who are able to walk in for treatment.

The level of education and training required to become a physician assistant or nurse will depend on the specialization that interests you. When choosing a field, you should first consider where your interests and talents lie. Do you like to work with people? Do you want to be able to work directly with patients and administer primary care? Are you interested in assisting with surgery, or are you more interested in educating and comforting patients and their families. What you find most appealing should help guide you to the right medical career for you. Whatever you choose, there are specific training and education requirements.

Physician Assistants

If you are interested in becoming a physician assistant, then your first step after graduating high school is to go to college. Though the requirements for admission to PA training programs vary, most applicants already have a college degree and some health-related work experience. In addition, many PAs have prior experience as registered nurses, emergency medical technicians, and paramedics. Every state requires that physician assistants complete an *accredited*, formal education program and pass a national exam to obtain a license.

Programs

Physician assistant educational programs usually take at least two years for full-time students to complete. Most programs are at schools of allied health, academic health centers, medical schools, or four-year colleges; others are at community colleges, are part of the military, or are at hospitals. Many accredited PA programs have *clinical* teaching relationships with medical schools.

If you are planning on applying to physician assistant programs, make sure the programs are accredited by the Accreditation Review Commission on Education for the Physician Assistant. According the Bureau of Labor Statistics, in 2008, 142 education programs for physician assistants were accredited or provisionally accredited by this commission. Eighty percent, or 113, of these programs offered the option of a *master's degree*, 21 of them offered a *bachelor's degree*, three awarded *associate's degrees*, and five awarded a certificate.

Before entering physician assistant programs, many people gain experience in health services through work as paramedics or nurses.

INSTRUCTION

Physician assistant education includes classroom and laboratory instruction in a variety of subjects, including biochemistry, pathology, human anatomy, physiology, clinical pharmacology, clinical medicine, physical diagnosis, and medical ethics. PA programs also include supervised clinical training in several different areas of medicine, including family medicine, internal medicine, surgery, prenatal care and gynecology, geriatrics, emergency medicine, and pediatrics. Sometimes, physician assistant students work in one or more of these areas under the supervision of a physician who is seeking to hire a PA. This position may lead to permanent employment in one of the areas where the student works.

LICENSURE

All states and the District of Columbia have laws that regulate the practice of physician assistants. All physician assistants must pass the Physician Assistant National Certifying Examination, administered by the National Commission on Certification of Physician Assistants (NCCPA) and open only to graduates of accredited PA education programs. Only if you successfully complete and pass the examination can you label yourself "Physician Assistant-Certified." To maintain certification, physician assistants must complete 100 hours of additional medical education every two years. Every six years, they must pass a recertification examination or complete an alternative program combining learning experiences and a take-home examination.

Advancement

As a physician assistant, you may choose to pursue additional education in a specialty. Postgraduate programs are available in areas such as internal medicine, rural primary care, emergency medicine, surgery, pediatrics, neonatology, and occupational medicine. To be accepted by one of these programs, you must be a graduate of an accredited program and be certified by the NCCPA.

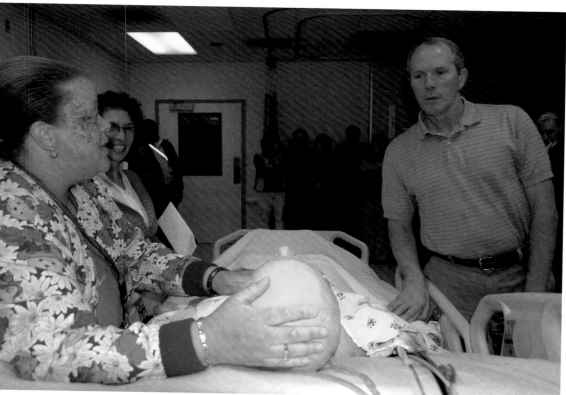

After receiving their degrees or certifications, nurses and physician assistants will need to undergo additional training and education.

As they gain more knowledge and experience, physician assistants are able to gain responsibilities and earn higher wages. However, physician assistants will always have to practice under the supervision of a doctor.

NURSES

Registered nurses may have a bachelor's degree, an associate degree, or a diploma from an approved nursing program. Nurses usually complete an associate degree or bachelor's degree program and then complete a national licensing examination in order to obtain a nursing license. Advanced practice nurses need a master's degree.

EDUCATION

There are three possible educational paths to become a registered nurse—a bachelor's of science degree in nursing (BSN), an associate's degree in nursing (ADN), and a diploma. BSN programs, offered by colleges and universities, take about four years to complete. ADN programs, offered by community and junior colleges, take about two to three years to complete. Diploma programs, administered in hospitals, last about three years. Licensed graduates of any of the three types of educational programs qualify for entry-level nursing positions. Diploma programs are less common than ADN or BSN programs.

If you are interested in nursing, you should carefully weigh the advantages and disadvantages of each type of education program. What are your ultimate career goals? Keep in mind that advancement opportunities may be more limited for ADN and diploma holders compared to nurses who obtain a BSN or higher. Individuals who complete a bachelor's degree receive more training in areas such as communication, leadership, and critical thinking, all of which are becoming more important as nursing becomes more complex. Additionally, bachelor's degree programs offer more clinical experience in nonhospital settings. A bachelor's or higher degree is often necessary if you are interested in administrative positions, research, consulting, or teaching.

Nursing students need to complete classroom instruction as well as hands-on training. This nursing student is working on a 200-hour training rotation at a hospital affiliated with her nursing program.

All these nursing education programs include classroom instruction and supervised clinical experience in hospitals and other facilities. Students take classroom courses in anatomy, physiology, microbiology, chemistry, nutrition, psychology, and nursing. ADN and BSN students will also take general *liberal arts* courses. Clinical experiences is gained in hospital departments such as pediatrics, psychiatry, maternity, and surgery, as well as in nursing care facilities, public health departments, home health agencies, and ambulatory clinics.

ADVANCING YOUR EDUCATION

If you choose to get an ADN or diploma, you can later enter a bachelor's degree program to advance your career. Many nurses

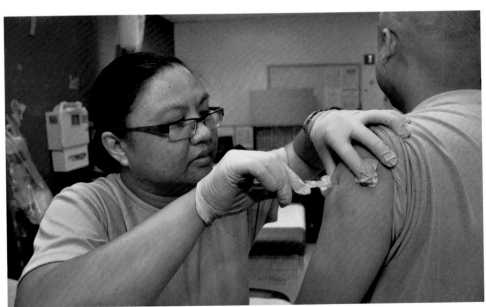

Captain Betty Ann Buentipo, whose story is told on the facing page, is a nurse in the Air Force Reserve.

Real-Life Nurse

Captain Betty Ann Buentipo, a reservist with the 724th Aeromedical Staging Flight at Anderson Air Force Base, had a grandmother who had always wanted to become a nurse but never had the money to pursue her dream. Betty Ann was the only other family member interested in nursing, and she promised her grandmother at her deathbed that she would become a nurse.

In 1999, while pursuing a bachelor in science nursing degree at the University of Guam, she began working as a nurse's aide at Guam Memorial Hospital. After graduating in 2000, she worked her way to becoming a nurse at GMH that same year. In 2007, inspired by her brother's service in the Air Force, she decided to join the Air Force Reserve and the 724th ASTF.

Captain Buentipo said her job at GMH calls for her to be more than an emergency room nurse. "I have to transition to becoming an ICU nurse, to being a pediatric nurse, to a surgical attendant to a telemetry nurse because there are no rooms, and we have to take care of all of these patients," she said.

In addition to these varied duties, Captain Buentipo also has to transition between working in the civilian sector and the military. Despite these challenges, she reminds her coworkers to treat all patients like they were their own family.

Caring for others was something Captain Buentipo got from her grandmother. "I think that she would be proud," said Captain Buentipo.

can find an entry-level position with an ADN or diploma and then take advantage of tuition reimbursement benefits to work toward a BSN by completing an RN-to-BSN program. Accelerated master's degree programs in nursing (MSN) also are available. These programs typically take a full-time student three to four years to complete and result in the award of both the BSN and MSN.

If you have already gotten a bachelor's degree in another field and then decide to enter nursing, there are accelerated BSN programs that help you achieve this in only 12 to 18 months. In addition there are two-year MSN programs available for individuals who hold a bachelor's or higher degree in another field.

LICENSURE

In the United States, students must graduate from an approved nursing program and pass a national licensing examination, known as the National Council Licensure Examination, or NCLEX-RN, in order to obtain a nursing license. Other eligibility requirements for licensure vary by state.

ADVANCEMENT

Most RNs begin as staff nurses in hospitals and, with experience and good performance, can be promoted to positions with more responsibility. In management, nurses can advance from assistant unit manager or head nurse to more senior-level administrative roles of assistant director, director, vice president, or chief of nursing. Increasingly, these management-level nursing positions require a graduate degree or an advanced degree in nursing or health services administration.

Some nurses choose to become advanced practice nurses, which require at least a master's degree. In addition, all states specifically define requirements for registered nurses in advanced practice roles. Advanced practice nurses may prescribe medicine, but the authority to prescribe varies by state.

Some nurses move into the business side of health care. Their nursing expertise and experience enable them to manage *ambulatory*, acute, home-based, and chronic care businesses. Employers—including hospitals, insurance companies, pharmaceutical manufacturers, and managed care organizations, among others—need RNs for health planning and development, marketing, consulting, policy development, and quality assurance. Other nurses work as college and university faculty or conduct research.

If You Have a Creative Personality . . .

You might be able to find ways to combine your artistic tendencies with a career in nursing. Music and art can be useful therapeutic tools for many groups of people (especially children and the elderly)—but keep in mind that the focus of a nursing career will not be the arts!

If You Have a Realistic Personality . . .

You may enjoy a career as either a PA or a nurse. Both careers will allow you to use practical tools you can see and touch to help people with their health issues.

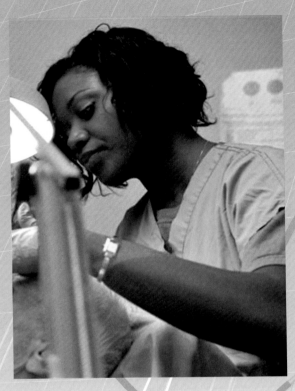

Don't give up. Believe in yourself and your purpose.

—Laurence G. Boldt

ABOUT THE QUOTE

If you have a career goal that excites you, believe in your ability to make it happen. As you talk to others in the field and gather more information, you may find that even seemingly impossible obstacles turn out to not be as great as you first thought. Don't be afraid to take chances sometimes!

CHAPTER 4
JOB OPPORTUNITIES AND RELATED OCCUPATIONS

WORDS TO KNOW

auditory: Having to do with hearing or the parts of the body that help you hear, such as the ears.
sensory: Having to do with the senses.
neural: Having to do with the nerves.
cognitive: Related to thinking and the mental processes that go on in your brain, such as memory, reasoning, and perception.
fluency: The ability to speak smoothly and easily.

So you've decided to become a physician assistant or nurse, and you've started down the appropriate education path. What happens after graduation or the completion of training? Will there be jobs available? Where are they and how will you find them?

JOB OPPORTUNITIES

Over the next decade, job opportunities are expected to be excellent for physician assistants and nurses.

Physician Assistants

According to the Bureau of Labor Statistics, in 2008, physician assistants held about 74,800 jobs. This number is actually higher than the number of practicing PAs because many physician assistants hold more than one job. For example, some PAs work with a supervising physician but also work in another healthcare facility.

Did You Know?

According to the American Academy of Physician Assistants, in 2008, about 15 percent of actively practicing PAs worked in more than one clinical job at the same time.

More than 53 percent of jobs for PAs were in the offices of physicians. About 24 percent were in general medical and surgical hospitals. The rest were mostly in outpatient care centers, the federal government, and public or private colleges, universities, and professional schools.

Nurses

As the largest health-care occupation, registered nurses held about 2.6 million jobs in 2008; 60 percent of these were at hospitals. About 8 percent of jobs were in offices of physicians, 5 percent in home health-care services, 5 percent in nursing care facilities, and 3 percent in employment services. The remainder worked mostly in government agencies, social assistance agencies, and educational services.

Related Occupations

Perhaps you are interested in medicine, but none of the nursing or physician assistant positions sound just right. You might want to consider another related job.

AUDIOLOGISTS

Audiologists work with people who have hearing, balance, and related ear problems. They examine individuals of all ages and identify those with the symptoms of hearing loss and other *auditory*, balance, and related *sensory* and *neural* problems. They then assess the nature and extent of the problems and help the individuals manage them.

OCCUPATIONAL THERAPISTS

Occupational therapists help patients improve their ability to perform tasks in living and working environments. They work with

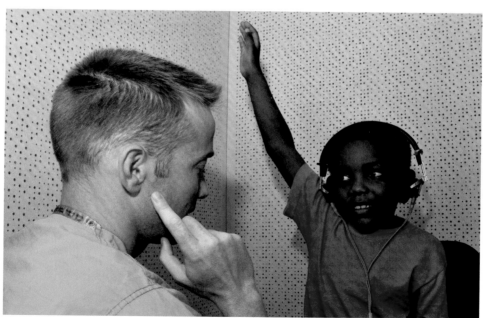

Johnny Foster, an Air Force audiologist, performs a hearing test on a Guyanese boy as part of New Horizons Guyana 2009. New Horizons Guyana is an annual humanitarian assistance program aiding the countries of Latin America and the Caribbean.

individuals who suffer from a mentally, physically, developmentally, or emotionally disabling condition. Occupational therapists use treatments to develop, recover, or maintain the daily living and work skills of their patients. The goal is to help clients have independent, productive, and satisfying lives.

PHYSICAL THERAPISTS

Physical therapists, sometimes referred to as simply PTs, are health-care professionals who diagnose and treat individuals of all ages who have injuries or other health-related conditions that limit their abilities to move. Physical therapists examine each

Physical therapist Marta Bloyer helps an earthquake survivor walk in Port-au-Prince, Haiti.

individual and develop a plan using treatment techniques to promote the ability to move, reduce pain, restore function, and prevent further disability.

SPEECH-LANGUAGE PATHOLOGISTS

Speech-language pathologists, sometimes called speech therapists, assess, diagnose, treat, and help to prevent disorders related to speech, language, *cognitive*-communication, voice, swallowing, and *fluency*.

DENTAL HYGIENISTS

Dental hygienists examine patients' teeth and gums, remove soft and hard deposits from teeth, teach patients how to practice good oral hygiene, and provide other preventive dental care.

DIAGNOSTIC MEDICAL SONOGRAPHERS

Diagnostic medical sonographers use special equipment to direct high-frequency sound waves into areas of the patient's body. Sonographers operate the equipment, which collects reflected echoes and forms an image that may be videotaped, transmitted, or photographed for interpretation and diagnosis by a physician.

EMERGENCY MEDICAL TECHNICIANS AND PARAMEDICS

EMTs and paramedics care for and transport the sick or injured to a medical facility in the case of an emergency like a car accident, heart attack, or gunshot wound.

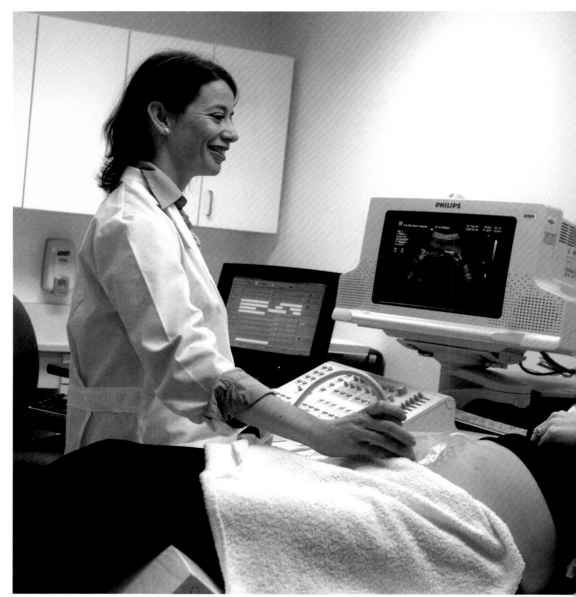

Sifa Turan, sonographer at Yale Ob/Gyn, consults with a patient on an ultrasound. Ultrasounds, or sonograms, are routine tests done during pregnancy to check on fetal development and growth.

LICENSED PRACTICAL AND LICENSED VOCATIONAL NURSES

Licensed practical nurses (LPNs) or licensed vocational nurses (LVNs) work under the direction of physicians and registered nurses. They care for patients who are sick, injured, recovering from illness or surgery, or disabled.

If You Have an Investigative Personality . . .

You might enjoy putting your skills to work to find practical answers to health problems. As a nurse or PA, you will have some opportunities to use math and science in your work, which you will enjoy. However, a job in medical research might be more suited to your interests and talents.

The best preparation for good work tomorrow is to do good work today.

—Ebert Hubbard

ABOUT THE QUOTE

You may feel as though your adult career still lies far in the future. But right now is the bridge that leads into the future. By consistently doing good work wherever you are now—today in high school, again when you are in college, then when you land your first entry-level position, and so on through the rest of your life—you build the steps that will lead you to new opportunities.

CHAPTER 5
THE FUTURE FOR PAs AND NURSES

WORDS TO KNOW

subsidized: Paid for at least in part by another, often an employer or the government.
prospective: Referring to something that is potential or possible in the future.

In general, the job outlook for careers in the healthcare industry is excellent. In fact, the healthcare industry is predicted to add nearly 4 million new jobs between 2006 and 2016, and have the fastest annual growth rate of all career industries.

As the country's population ages, there is a rising need to fill many essential health-care positions. No matter the region of the country or the community, the need for skilled workers is expected to be high in all specialties within the health-care industry.

PHYSICIAN ASSISTANTS

At a projected growth rate of 39 percent, employment for physician assistants is projected to grow much faster than the 11 percent average for all occupations. This rapid growth is expected because of the expansion of health-care industries and an emphasis on lower costs, which will lead to an increasing use of physician assistants. PAs are cost effective because they can relieve more expensive physicians of routine duties and procedures. In addition, health-care providers will use more physician assistants as many states continue to expand PAs' scope of practice by allowing them to perform more procedures.

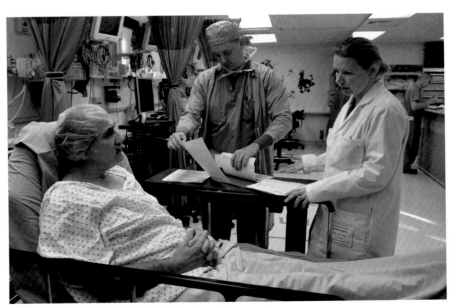

Who is the doctor and who is the nurse? In this image, the male nurse (in green scrubs) is assisting the female doctor (white coat). However, less than 10 percent of nurses in the United States are male.

Real-Life Physician Assistant

Teresa Holler always wanted to work in medicine. After a college internship at a hospital opened her eyes to the long hours worked by physicians, she decided that a career as a doctor wasn't for her. She wanted a career that would still give her time for family. She did some research and ended up in a two-year physician assistant program.

She now has twelve years of experience as a physician assistant and she has gone from working with a government agency treating under-served populations in North Carolina to working in a cardiology practice to now educating corporations and community groups about health and wellness.

She recommends that before entering a physician assistant program, students should get some experience being around patients—intern at a hospital, volunteer, or shadow a physician.

Besides jobs in traditional office-based settings, physician assistants should find a growing number of jobs in institutional settings such as hospitals, academic medical centers, public clinics, and prisons. Job opportunities should be good, especially in rural and inner-city clinics—settings that often have difficulty attracting physicians.

Nurses

Overall job opportunities for registered nurses are expected to be excellent. Over the next decade, employment of RNs is expected to grow at 22 percent, much faster than the average for other jobs. Because the occupation is already very large, 581,500 new jobs will result, among the largest number of new jobs for any occupation.

However, employment of registered nurses will not grow at the same rate in every industry. Employment is expected to grow slowest in hospitals and fastest in physician's offices. In addition, because of an increase in the number of older people requiring long-term care, job opportunities are expected to increase in nursing-care facilities and in home health-care services.

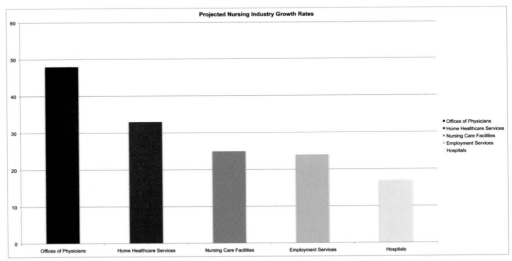

According to the Bureau of Labor Statistics, nursing is projected to be one of the fastest growing careers over the next decade. Many of these new positions will be in doctors' offices and home healthcare services.

Despite slower employment growth in hospitals, job opportunities should still be excellent because there is relatively high turnover among hospital nurses. To attract and retain qualified nurses, hospitals sometimes offer signing bonuses, family-friendly work schedules, or *subsidized* training. Although faster employment growth is projected in doctor's offices, nurses vying for these positions may face greater competition because these jobs generally offer regular hours and more comfortable working environments. Nurses with at least a bachelor's degree will have better job prospects than those without a bachelor's. In addition, all four advanced practice specialties—clinical nurse specialists, nurse practitioners, nurse-midwives, and nurse anesthetists—will be in high demand, particularly in inner cities and rural areas.

PLANNING FOR THE FUTURE

The information in this book is meant to be only an introduction to the health-care industry and to some of the career opportunities available for physician assistants and nurses. If you think you are interested in one of these health-care careers, it is never too early to start learning your options or to begin gaining experience.

• Speak to a school guidance counselor to get advice on how to find student jobs or educational opportunities in health care in your area.

• A guidance counselor might also be able to help you find an internship or a physician willing to let you shadow her or him.

- Volunteer at a hospital, nursing home, or other health-care facility. Getting the chance to see nurses and physician assistants in action, and actually interacting with patients yourself will help you learn if you would enjoy a career in health care.

- Find out if your high school or town offers training in first aid or emergency services. After some training, you may even be able to volunteer with your local fire department or ambulance squad.

Everything you do that is related to your interest in a health-care career will help guide you to the specialization for which you are most suited and will strengthen you in the eyes of *prospective* schools or employers.

If You Have an Enterprising Personality . . .

You might enjoy a management position in nursing. In a job like this you would have plenty of chances to let your energetic, sociable, and ambitious nature shine, and your abilities to be a leader would make you an effective supervisor for other nurses. Remember, though, that as a nurse or PA, you will always report at some level to a doctor—and, as with almost any career field, nursing requires that you begin at an entry level. Your dedication and good work at lower-level jobs are usually what allow you to work your way up to management-level positions.

FURTHER READING

Department of Economic and Social Affairs—Population Division. *World Population Ageing: 1950–2050.* New York: United Nations, 2002.

Novotny, Jeanne M., PhD, RN, FAAN; Doris Lippman, EdD, APRN, CS; Nicole Sanders, BSN, RN; and Joyce Fitzpatrick, PhD, MBA, RN, FAAN. *101 Careers in Nursing.* New York: Springer Publishing Company, Inc., 2003.

Rodican, Andrew. *Getting Into the Physician Assistant School of Your Choice.* New York: McGraw-Hill Companies, 2004.

Shakur, Rameen. *A Career in Medicine: Do You Have What It Takes?* London: Royal Society of Medicine Press, 2007.

Stanfield, Peggy S. *Introduction to the Health Professions, Fourth Edition.* Sudbury, Mass.: Jones and Bartlett Publishers, 2002.

FIND OUT MORE ON THE INTERNET

Accreditation Review Commission on Education for the Physician Assistants
www.arc-pa.org

American Academy of Physician Assistants Information Center
www.aapa.org

American Association of Colleges of Nursing
www.aacn.nche.edu

American Nurses Association
nursingworld.org

Career Compass
www.careervoyages.gov/careercompass-main.cfm

National Commission on Certification of Physician Assistants, Inc.
www.nccpa.net

National League for Nursing
www.nln.org

DISCLAIMER

The websites listed on this page were active at the time of publication. The publisher is not responsible for websites that have changed their address or discontinued operation since the date of publication. The publisher will review and update the websites upon each reprint.

BIBLIOGRAPHY

Bureau of Labor Statistics. "Physician Assistants," www.bls.gov/oco/ocos081.htm (15 April 2010).

Bureau of Labor Statistics. "Registered Nurses," www.bls.gov/oco/ocos083.htm (15 April 2010).

National Center for Research Resources. "Consortium Directory," www.ncrr.nih.gov/clinical_research_resources/clinical_and_translational_science_awards/consortium_directory (23 April 2010).

National Institute on Aging. *Why Population Aging Matters: A Global Perspective.* National Institutes of Health, Publication No. 07-6134, March 2007.

Salary Stories. "Physician Assistant Salaries: A Day in the Life of a Physician Assistant," blogs.payscale.com/salarystories/2007/09/physician-assis.html (23 April 2010).

United States Air Force. "Nurse Serves Two Worlds in Guam," www. afrc.af.mil/news/story.asp?id=123158673 (25 April 2010).

United States Census Bureau. "Census Bureau Reports World's Older Population Projected to Triple by 2050," www.census.gov/Press-Release/www/releases/archives/international_population/013882. html (23 April 2010).

United States Department of Health and Human Services. "A Profile of Older Americans: 2009," www.aoa.gov/AoARoot/Aging_Statistics/ Profile/2009/3.aspx (23 April 2010).

United States Department of Health and Human Services. "Changing Demographics and the Implications for Physicians, Nurses and Other Health Workers," www.bhpr.hrsa.gov/healthworkforce/reports/ changedemo/aging.htm (23 April 2010).

World Health Organization. "Ageing," www.who.int/topics/ageing/en/ (23 April 2010).

World Health Organization. "Our Ageing World," www.who.int/ageing/en/index.html (23 April 2010).

INDEX

United States Bureau of Labor Statistics 11
United States Census Bureau 25
United States Department of Health and Human Services 30

Volunteer 55, 58

World Health Organization 25

PICTURE CREDITS

Creative Commons Attribution
    isafmedia: pg. 13

Creative Commons Attribution-Share Alike 3.0 Unported
    Loren Cobb: pg. 24

Fotolia.com
    Andrea Biraghi: pg. 35
    Astoria: pg. 11
    Dmitry Nikolaev: pg. 32
    midwestgal: pg. 8
    Sandor Kacso: pg. 22
    Yuri Arcurs: pg. 52

United States Air Force: pg. 41
    Perry Aston: pg. 47
    Suzanne M. Day: pp. 17, 19

United States Navy
    Joan E. Kretschmer: pg. 48

Yale University: pg. 50

To the best knowledge of the publisher, all images not specifically credited are in the public domain. If any image has been inadvertently uncredited, please notify Harding House Publishing Service, 220 Front Street, Vestal, New York 13850, so that credit can be given in future printings.

ABOUT THE AUTHOR

Cordelia Strange has a master's degree from Binghamton University and is especially interested in health, the environment, and education. She enjoys applying these interests (and others) in writing books for young people.

ABOUT THE CONSULTANT

Michael Puglisi is the director of the Department of Labor's Workforce New York One Stop Center in Binghamton, New York. He has also held several leadership positions in the International Association of Workforce Professionals (IAWP), a non-profit educational association exclusively dedicated to workforce professionals with a rich tradition and history of contributions to workforce excellence. IAWP members receive the tools and resources they need to effectively contribute to the workforce development system daily. By providing relevant education, timely and informative communication and valuable findings of pertinent research, IAWP equips its members with knowledge, information and practical tools for success. Through its network of local and regional chapters, IAWP is preparing its members for the challenges of tomorrow.